SCIENCE
QUESTIONS & ANSWERS

Indoor Science

Anita Ganeri

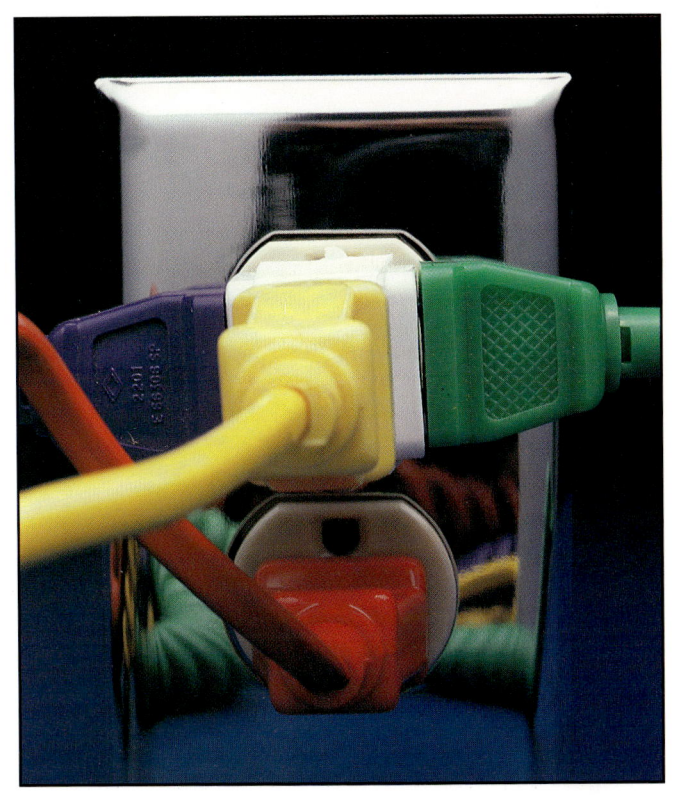

Evans Brothers Limited

Published by Evans Brothers Limited
2A Portman Mansions
Chiltern Street
London W1M 1LE

First published 1993

Printed in Hong Kong

ISBN 0 237 51248 3

Acknowledgements

The author and publishers would like to thank the following
for her valuable help and advice:
Sally Morgan MA, MSc, MIBiol

Illustrations: Virginia Gray - pages 19, 28, 41, 42, 45
Jillian Luff of Bitmap Graphics - pages 6, 17, 30, 31
Editors: Catherine Chambers and Jean Coppendale
Design: Monica Chia
Production: Peter Thompson

For permission to reproduce copyright material the author
and publishers gratefully acknowledge the following:
-
page 6 - Garry Gay, The Image Bank; page 7 - (top left) Martyn F Chillmaid, Robert Harding Picture Library, (top right) Max Schneider, The Image Bank, (bottom) Oscar Burriel, Science Photo Library; page 8 - Robert Harding Picture Library; page 9 - (top right) Martyn F Chillmaid, Robert Harding Picture Library, (bottom right) Sally Morgan, Ecoscene, (bottom left) Walter Iooss Jr, The Image Bank; page 10 - Sally Morgan, Ecoscene; page 11 - (top) Phil Jude, Science Photo Library, (bottom) Robert Harding Picture Library; page 12 - John Hatt, The Hutchison Library; page 13 - (top left) Sally Morgan, Ecoscene, (top right) Paul Trummer, The Image Bank, (bottom right) Vaughan Fleming, Science Photo Library; page 14 - (inset) Arthur Meyerson, The Image Bank, (main picture) Zefa; page 15 - (bottom left) Romilly Lockyer, The Image Bank, (top right) Sally Morgan, Ecoscene, (bottom right) Anthony Cooper, Ecoscene; page 16 - (top left) David Guyon, Science Photo Library, (bottom left) Lorenzo Lees, Ecoscene; page 17 - (bottom left) Sally Morgan, Ecoscene, (top right) Nils Jorgensen, Rex Features; page 18 - (top) Geoff du Feu, Planet Earth Pictures, (bottom left) Last Resort Picture Agency, (bottom right) Zefa; page 19 - (top) Last Resort Picture Agency, (middle) Ever Ready Ltd; page 20 - (left) Richard Megna, Fundamental Photos, Science Photo Library, (right) Courtesy of the Institution of Electrical Engineers; page 21 - (left) Kim Taylor, Bruce Coleman Ltd, (middle right) Lou Jones, The Image Bank, (bottom right) Bruce Coleman Ltd; page 22 - (left) Garry Gay, The Image Bank, (right) Bill Varie, The Image Bank; page 23 - (left) Sally Morgan, Ecoscene, (middle right) Dr Jeremy Burgess, Science Photo Library, (bottom) Sally Morgan, Ecoscene; page 24 - (left) Norman Tomalin, Bruce Coleman Ltd, (right) Gisela Caspersen, The Image Bank; page 25 - Zefa; page 26 - (top) Adrienne Hart-Davis, Science Photo Library, (bottom) Gerhard Gscheidle, The Image Bank; page 27 - (top) Adrienne Hart-Davis, Science Photo Library, (bottom) Sally Morgan, Ecoscene; page 28 - Robert Harding Picture Library; page 29 - (top) Sally Morgan, Ecoscene, (middle left) Robert Harding Picture Library, (middle right) Zefa; page 30 - Derik Murray Photography, The Image Bank; page 31 - (left) Sally Morgan, Ecoscene, (right) The Image Bank; page 32 - Sally Morgan, Ecoscene; page 33 - (left) Gray Mortimore, Allsport, (right) Robert Harding Picture Library; page 34 - (top) Colin Molineux, The Image Bank, (bottom) John Kelly, The Image Bank; page 35 - (left) Adam Hart-Davis, Science Photo Library, (right) Last Resort Picture Library; page 36 - (middle) Max Schneider, The Image Bank, (bottom) Zefa; page 37 - (top) Robert Harding Picture Library, (middle) Sally Morgan, Ecoscene, (bottom) Dr Jeremy Burgess, Science Photo Library; page 38 - (left) Adam Hart-Davis, Science Photo Library, (right) Sally Morgan, Ecoscene; page 39 - (top) Sobel Klonsky, The Image Bank, (bottom) Sally Morgan, Ecoscene; page 40 - Sally Morgan, Ecoscene; page 41 - (left) Robert Harding Picture Library, (right) Jon Davison, Stockphotos; page 42 - Sally Morgan, Ecoscene; page 43 - Sally Morgan, Ecoscene; page 44 - (left) Alex Bartel, Science Photo Library, (right) Robert Harding Picture Library; page 45 - Robert Harding Picture Library

Contents

The words in **bold** in the text are explained in the Glossary on page 46.

What is the difference between ice and water?

Water and ice are two very different substances which you can see in the kitchen. But did you know that although ice and water do not look like each other, they are both different forms of water? Most of the things around you, such as water and metals, can exist in three forms – as solids, liquids or gases. These three forms are called the three states of matter. Ice is the solid form of the liquid, water. The gas form of water is water **vapour**.

All the things around you are made up of tiny particles, called molecules. They are much too small to see. The molecules themselves are made of even tinier particles, called atoms. The different states of matter are caused by the different ways in which molecules in a substance are grouped together.

In a solid substance, the molecules are very close together. They are kept in a fixed shape by very strong **bonds**. In a liquid, the molecules are still quite close together but the bonds between them are not so strong. This is why liquids can flow and change shape. Look at a glass of water – the liquid has taken the shape of its container. In a gas, the bonds are looser still. The molecules move around freely, allowing the gas to spread out.

Solid molecules are close together.

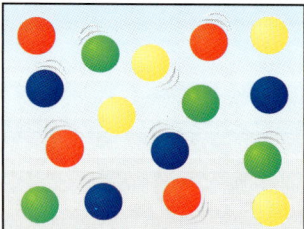
Liquid molecules move further apart.

Gas molecules move around freely.

The three states of matter.

Water in its liquid state.

Why is syrup difficult to pour?

All liquids flow but some flow more easily than others. This is why it is easier to pour water or milk than syrup or honey. The thickness and stickiness of a liquid is called its viscosity. The thicker a liquid, the more viscous it is.

Left: Water flows freely because it is not very viscous.

Right: Milk is more viscous than water.

Sticky syrup is very viscous.

How does water change to ice?

When you take ice cubes out of the fridge, you probably do not stop to think how flowing water has changed to solid ice. Things change from one state of matter to another when they are heated or cooled.

If you heat ice (solid water), it turns into liquid water. This process is called melting. If you heat the liquid further, it will turn into water vapour (gas). This is called evaporation. If water vapour is cooled down, it turns back into liquid water. This is called

As the ice warms up, it melts into water.

condensation. If liquid is cooled down further, it turns into solid ice. This is called freezing.

Things change from solids, to liquids, to gases when they are heated because the heat makes their molecules move faster and loosens the bonds between them. They change from gases, to liquids, to solids when they are cooled because the molecules slow down and

the bonds get firmer as the heat is taken away.

Different substances change from one state of matter to another at different temperatures. Ice melts at 0° C, which is its melting point. It boils and turns into water vapour at 100° C. This is its boiling point. As the water vapour cools below 100° C, it turns back (condenses) into liquid water again. Water turns to ice at 0° C. This is its freezing point.

How do ice cubes cool drinks down?

If you put ice cubes into a drink, they cool it down as they melt. This is because the ice uses heat energy in order to melt. It takes this energy from the drink itself and so the drink becomes cooler. The drink also gets cooler because of the cold water produced as the ice melts.

Ice cubes are cooling these drinks down.

What makes a fridge keep things cold?

There is a system of pipes inside a fridge which carries a special chemical liquid around it. As the liquid passes through the inside of the fridge, it changes to vapour. To do this, it uses energy in the form of heat. The heat is taken from the air around the pipes, which in turn draws it from the food inside the fridge, cooling everything down. The heat is passed out at the back of the fridge. If you put your hand near the back of your fridge, you should feel heat coming from it.

Stocking up the fridge.

Did you know?

If you put pressure on ice, you raise its freezing point. This means that the outer layer stays liquid for a longer time. This is how ice skates work. As you skate, your weight presses down on the blades and on the ice. This extra pressure stops the ice freezing so that there is a thin film of water under each skate. The water does not grip your skate blades as strongly as ice. So you can skate more easily.

Skaters can move very fast across the ice.

Why does sugar dissolve in a hot drink?

When you put sugar into a hot drink, it disappears quickly and mixes with the liquid. The sugar is dissolved in the liquid. Most solid substances dissolve better in hot liquids than in cold ones. This is because the heat from the hot drink makes the molecules of sugar spread out and move around. The sugar will dissolve even more quickly if you stir the hot drink.

The sugar will dissolve quickly in the coffee, especially if it is stirred.

When you dissolve something in a liquid, you form a solution. So if you dissolve salt in water, you make a salt solution. If a substance is able to dissolve in water, it is called soluble. Salt and sugar are both soluble. If a substance does not dissolve in water, it is called insoluble. Sand is insoluble; so is chalk.

When does water stop dissolving solids?

Start adding some salt to a glass of warm water. There will come a point when no more salt will dissolve in the water. You will see grains of salt sinking to the bottom of the glass because the water cannot hold any more salt. The glass now contains what is called a saturated solution. The hotter the water, the more salt will dissolve in it before the solution becomes saturated. If you leave the solution to cool down, the salt molecules will join up again and you will be able to see the salt crystals once more.

 See for yourself

Try this experiment to see how well different solids dissolve in hot or cold liquids. See how much sugar or salt you can dissolve in warm and then cold water. Add the sugar or salt a teaspoonful at a time. Does it dissolve more quickly in the warm water or the cold water? Does it dissolve more quickly if you stir it? Try other solids such as the ones shown in the picture below.

Try dissolving some of these substances in water: chilli pepper, black pepper, curry powder, flour, sugar, baking powder and coffee granules.

Why are fizzy drinks fizzy?

Gases also dissolve in liquids. Drinks such as lemonade are fizzy because they have carbon dioxide gas dissolved in them. The gas is bubbled into the liquid at the drinks' factory. It is bubbled in under pressure because gases dissolve better at higher pressure. When you take the top off a fizzy drinks' bottle, there is a hiss and fizz as the pressure **decreases** and some of the gas comes out of the liquid.

The gas molecules are spread out throughout the liquid. When they collect together, they form bubbles. If you put a drinking straw into some fizzy lemonade, you will be able to see the bubbles forming on the outside of the straw.

 DON'T see for yourself

Never shake a can or bottle of fizzy drink before you open it. The gas will collect at the top of the container and explode out, which could be dangerous.

Right: Drinks are given their fizz in this bottling factory.

Below: You can see the bubbles in this fizzy drink rising. Some are collecting on the slice of lemon.

Why do houses creak at night?

When you are in bed at night, do you ever hear strange creaking noises coming from your house? You are more likely to notice them after a warm summer's day. This is because things get slightly bigger when they get hot and shrink back to their normal size when they cool down again. These processes are called expansion and contraction.

During the day, the Sun heats the bricks and wood in your house. This makes them expand. At night, the temperature drops. The bricks and wood cool down and contract to their normal size again. As they do this, they rub against each other and you can hear them creaking. Things expand when they get warm because the heat makes their molecules move further apart, so they take up more space.

Why do doors jam?

On a hot day, the doors inside your house may jam or stick. This is because as they get hotter, the wood in them expands making them slightly bigger. The doors will open and close easily when they cool down and contract.

Tin roofs creak a lot at night because metal expands and contracts quickly as the temperature changes.

See for yourself

If you cannot unscrew the metal lid of a jar, run it under the hot tap for a few seconds. It should then undo quite easily. This is because metal expands more in the heat than glass does.

This lid will soon be able to unscrew.

Did you know?

Most central heating systems are controlled by a device called a thermostat. It automatically turns the heating off when the house is warm enough. Most thermostats are made up of two strips of different metals joined together. When they are heated, the two metals expand at different rates. This makes the whole strip bend and switch the heating system off. As the house gets cooler, the strip contracts. It then bends back again and turns the heating back on.

See for yourself

To see how water expands as it freezes, fill a plastic bottle with water and put it in the freezer. Leave it until the water is frozen solid. As the ice expands, it will crack the bottle. Never use a glass bottle!

Why do pipes burst in winter?

Most things expand as they heat up, but water expands as it cools down. Ice takes up more space than liquid water. If the water pipes in your house get very cold in winter, the water inside them may freeze. As it turns into ice, the water expands and can crack the pipes. The problem is made worse when the temperature rises and the ice melts. Then the water may leak out and cause a flood.

Above: Frozen icicles dangling down the outside of a house.

Right: The stream of water from this drainage pipe has frozen into solid ice.

How does washing-up liquid get plates clean?

Washing-up liquid works by removing the sticky grease and oil from dirty plates and cutlery, pots and pans. If you hold a greasy plate under a tap, the water will just run off it, leaving the droplets of grease behind. If you add some washing-up liquid to the water, it will take the grease with it. This is because washing-up liquid contains a special substance, called a detergent.

Detergents contain special chemicals. The molecules of these chemicals float around the water in groups. When they come across a globule of grease, they attach themselves to it and lift it off the plate. They surround the grease so that it is trapped and cannot get back on to the plate again. The molecules have long 'tails' which hate water. They bury into the grease and pull it away so that they, too, can get out of the water. Grease is removed faster in hot water. Why do you think this is so? Turn back to page 9 if you cannot guess.

Left: Bubbles of washing-up liquid.

Below: A lot of washing-up liquid has been used to get these glasses and plates clean.

Oil and grease do not normally mix in water. If you pour a small amount of cooking oil into a glass of water, you will see that the oil and water will not mix together, even if you give them a good stir. Now add a few drops of washing-up liquid. The detergent should make the oil dissolve in the water.

How do towels get you dry?

When you get out of the bath or shower, you use a towel to dry yourself. But do you know how the towel dries your skin? It is because of a process called capillary action. A towel is made up of lots of fluffy **fibres**. When it comes into contact with water, the water is pulled into the tiny spaces between the fibres. It is sucked into the towel, and away from your skin.

Towelling has a lot of fluffy fibres in it.

To see how capillary action works, you will need two clear plastic rulers and a saucer filled with coloured water. You can colour the water with food dye. Hold the rulers close together and stand them in the saucer. You should soon see the water rising slowly between them.

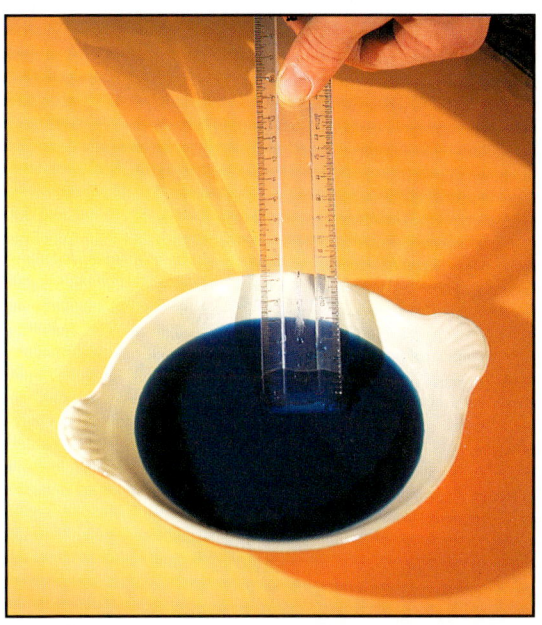

Capillary action also works in plant stems. Here, the flowers have turned blue because blue dye has been sucked up the stems.

What is electricity?

Electricity is a type of energy. We use it to power lots of the things in our homes, such as televisions, electric kettles, computers, hi-fis and lights. Have a look around your house – you might be surprised at how many things need electricity to make them work.

Most offices have a lot of electrical equipment, such as computers and fax machines.

How many electrical gadgets can you see in this kitchen? What are they used for?

Electricity is made by tiny particles, called electrons. These are found inside atoms (see page 7). The electrons carry an electric charge. There are two main types of electricity: static electricity and current electricity.

Why do your clothes crackle when you undress?

Do your clothes ever make a crackling sound when you take them off? Do they sparkle in the dark? Or does your hair crackle when you comb it? This crackling is caused by tiny sparks of electricity, called static electricity. When some types of material rub together, electrons move from one surface to another. The electrons are knocked off the atoms of one surface and then stick on to the atoms of the other. If one surface has many more electrons than the other, some of the electrons jump back on to the other surface again, to balance things out. This is what makes the sparks of electricity.

 Did you know?

Static electricity gets its name because it flashes in one place. It does not flow from place to place, like current electricity (see page 17). Lightning is caused by giant sparks of the same type of static electricity that comes off your clothes.

Did you know?

Photocopiers use static electricity to make them work. A large drum inside the photocopier attracts ink to it by static electricity. The ink is then transferred to a piece of paper so that it exactly copies the original picture or writing.

The piece of paper will be placed face down on to a sheet of glass on the photocopier.

 See for yourself

Rub a blown-up balloon on your clothes, and place the rubbed side against a wall. The balloon should stick to the wall. This is because electrons jump from your clothes to the balloon, leaving it charged with static electricity. Then, when you hold the balloon against the wall, electrons jump between the two, making them stick together. This works best with man-made materials such as polyester.

This balloon is held on to the wall by static electricity.

What happens when you plug in an electric kettle?

When you plug in and switch on an electric **appliance**, such as a kettle or a radio, electricity flows into it through wires in the wall socket and in the plug. Your kettle can now work. This type of flowing electricity is called current electricity. An electric current can only flow around an unbroken wire, called a circuit. If the circuit is broken, the electricity will not flow.

It is amazing to think that the electricity you use for your kettle is

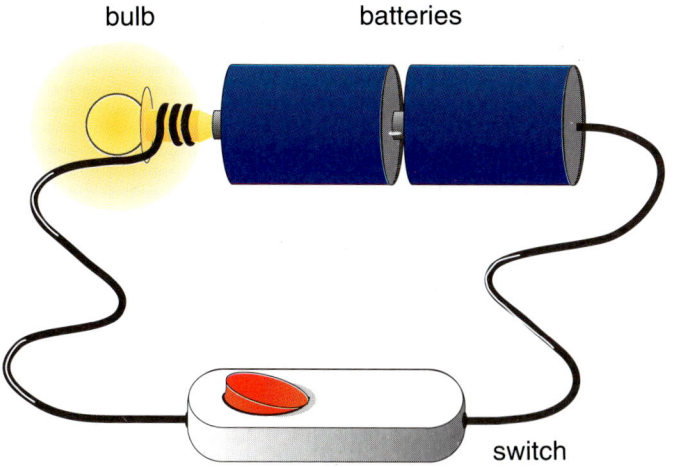

When the switch is turned on, the circuit is complete and the electricity can flow.

Electric cables are often strung along overhead pylons before they go underground.

made in a power station which may be far away from where you live. It travels to your home along wires that are threaded through cables. First, these cables are carried by tall pylons. Then they run underground into your house. Wires carry the electricity into the wall socket. There are wires in the plug as

This is a small petrol-powered generator which can make electricity for the home.

well. When you put the plug in and switch on the socket, you complete the circuit and the electricity can flow. When you switch the socket off, you break the circuit again.

 Did you know?

An electric current is measured in units, called amperes, or amps. The amount of electricity that an appliance such as a kettle uses up in a set time is measured in watts.

How does an electric kettle boil water?

When you plug an electric kettle in and switch it on, you complete a circuit. Electricity flows into the kettle where there is a special heater element. This gets hotter and hotter, heating the water inside the kettle until it boils. Most kettles also have a safety device called a circuit breaker. It makes the kettle switch off when the water reaches boiling point.

For safety, water must cover the heater element inside the kettle before it is switched on.

Electricity is very useful, but it can also be extremely dangerous. An electric shock can kill. Never play around with plugs or electrical appliances and never use a hairdryer or a kettle if you have got wet hands. Electricity flows through water very easily.

This sign on some electrical appliances warns of the danger of electricity.

What does a battery do?

Torches need electricity to make them work. But you do have to plug them in. They contain their own small stores of electricity in the form of batteries. A battery contains special chemicals. When you switch the torch on and complete the circuit inside it, these chemicals are converted into electrical energy. The battery acts like a pump and pushes the electricity around the circuit to make the light bulb work.

Torches can carry different types of battery.

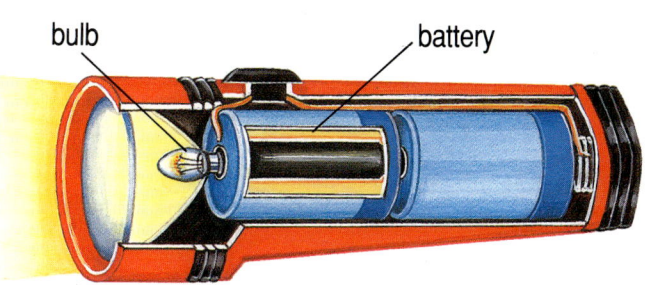

bulb   battery

The batteries inside the torch are stores of electricity.

 Did you know?

The electricity made by a battery flows one way around a circuit. But the mains electricity, which comes through sockets, changes direction all the time.

What makes a light bulb light up?

The hot filament inside the light bulb is glowing.

Before light bulbs were invented, people used first candles, and then gas-burning or oil-burning lamps to light up their homes. Today, all we have to do is go into a room and press a switch to turn the lights on.

Inside a light bulb, there is a coil of thin wire called a filament. It is normally made of the metal, tungsten. When you turn the light switch on, electricity flows through the wire. It makes the wire so hot that it glows brightly and gives out light. Tungsten metal is used in filaments because it does not melt when it gets very hot. It can reach a temperature of 2,500°C.

In a light bulb, electrical energy is changed into light and heat energy. Although light bulbs give out light, most of the electrical energy is turned into heat. Never touch a light bulb if it has just been on – you may get burnt.

Why do lights sometimes flicker?

The electricity that powers a light bulb is mains electricity, which is made in a power station. If something goes wrong at the power station, or if high winds blow the overhead cables about, the electricity supply can get weaker. This may make the lights in your house flicker for a short time. If there is a more serious problem, or if the cables snap in the wind, the electric current is broken. There may then be a longer power cut which lasts until repairs can be carried out.

 Did you know?

The first light bulb was invented by Thomas Edison in 1879. You can see it below. A modern light bulb usually lasts for about 750 hours. But people think that a light bulb in California has been giving out light since 1901.

Did you know?

Glow-worms and fireflies can make their own light. This helps them to signal to each other and recognize each other in the dark. It is also useful for attracting a mate.

Why do plugs have fuses?

If you take a three-pin plug apart and look inside, you will see that it contains a fuse and either two or three wires. The fuse is a safety device. If too much electricity flows through the plug, the plug can get too hot and even blow up. A fuse is made of a special type of metal which melts when it gets too hot. This breaks the circuit so that no more electricity can flow into the plug.

In a plug with three wires, the wires are called live, neutral and earth. The live and neutral wires carry the electricity to and from the appliance. The earth wire is another safety

device. If something goes wrong with the circuit, the earth wire will carry the electricity down in the ground to stop it causing any damage.

In a plug with two wires, there is no earth wire and no fuse. When an appliance or the circuit is faulty, it triggers a circuit breaker, which cuts off the electricity supply.

Two-pin plugs in a socket.

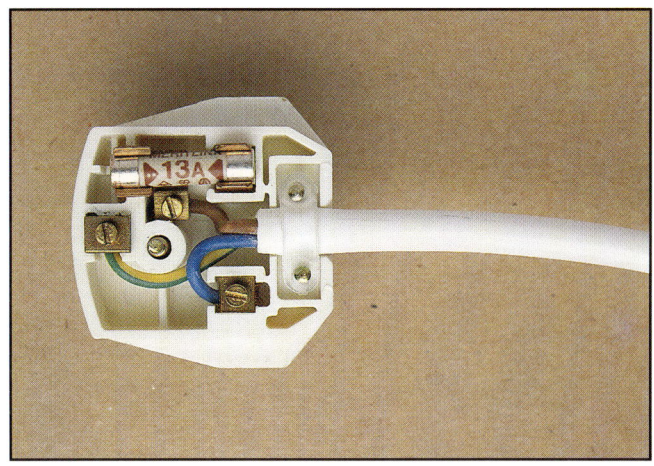

The inside of a three-pin plug, showing its fuse and wires.

How does a telephone work?

Sound is a form of energy. Sounds are made when something **vibrates** and causes the air around it to vibrate as well. The vibrations travel through the air as sound waves, making the sounds that you hear. When you speak, air rushes past your vocal cords in your throat. As your vocal cords vibrate, they make the air around them vibrate as well, so that your voice can be heard. Sound waves travel through the air like ripples through water. Your ears pick up the vibrations caused by the sound waves.

When you want to talk to someone on the telephone, you speak into a mouthpiece. Inside is a microphone, which contains a special device that vibrates as the sound waves hit it. It then turns the sound waves into electrical energy. The electrical signals travel along wires to the telephone exchange. Then they travel along another wire to the person you are calling. In the telephone earpiece, there is a loudspeaker. It contains a device which vibrates as the electrical signals hit it, making the air around it vibrate and produce sound. So the electrical signals are changed back into sound waves, which the person holding the receiver hears as words.

Telephones come in many shapes and sizes.

Thousands of wires inside a telephone exchange.

See for yourself

To see how sound is caused by vibrating air, try this experiment. You will need a jam jar, a piece of balloon, some shiny foil paper and a torch. Stretch the balloon across the top of the jar and if necessary hold it in place with an elastic band. Stick the foil on top of the balloon. Shine the torch at the foil and speak at it. The reflected beam should make a pattern as you speak.

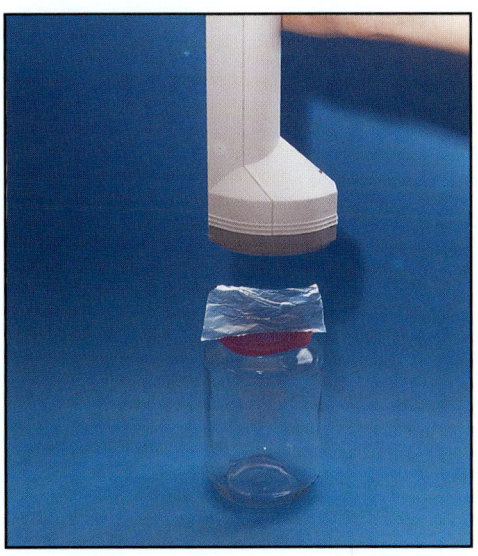

 ## Did you know?

The telephone was invented by Alexander Graham Bell in 1876. Today, there are about 425 million telephones in the world. In the USA, a staggering 422,000 million telephone calls are made each year.

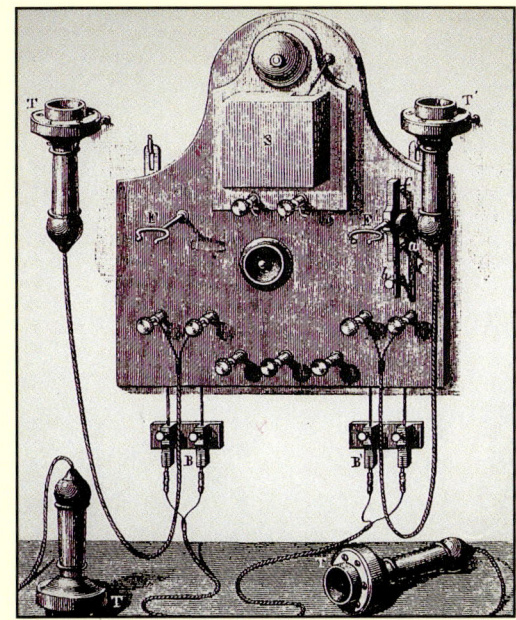

The telephone system developed by Alexander Graham Bell.

 ## See for yourself

You can make your own simple telephone with two yoghurt pots and a long piece of string. Make a small hole in the base of each pot, poke the ends of the string through and tie a knot so that the string cannot pull through the hole. Keep the string fairly **taut**. You can then speak into one pot, while a friend listens through the other. Your voice will make the air in the pot vibrate, which in turn will make the bottom of the pot vibrate. This will keep pulling and releasing the string, which will make the bottom of the pot at the other end vibrate, causing the air inside the pot to vibrate and produce sound.

Vibrating air produces sound inside the pot.

Why can you see yourself in a mirror?

Light travels in straight lines called light rays. We see things because light rays from the Sun or from electric lights bounce off objects and into our eyes. This is known as reflection. Light behaves a bit like a ball. If it hits something straight on, it bounces straight back off it. If it hits something at an angle, it bounces off at the same angle.

Light rays bounce off a smooth surface better than off a rough surface. A mirror has a very smooth surface which reflects light so well that light bounces straight back off it. Mirrors can be made of glass with a special silver coating on the back, or they can be made of polished metal. When you look at yourself in a mirror, light bounces off you and on to the mirror. It then bounces straight back into your eyes. This is how you see your reflection.

Why do you look the wrong way round in a mirror?

Light is bounced straight off a mirror, in exactly the same way as it hit it, because a mirror has such a smooth surface. This is how you see an exact reflection of yourself. The reflected rays make the parts of your body appear in exactly the same positions as they really are. So your head appears at the top, your feet at the bottom, your left hand on the left and your right hand on the right. But the **image** looks reversed because you are facing it.

A reflection of a building in the mirrored windows of a tower block.

This woman's right arm is reflected as her left arm in the mirror.

See for yourself

If you look at some writing in the mirror, it looks the wrong way round. Look at this piece of mirror writing. Can you read what it says? Now look at it in a mirror. You will be able to see it the right way round. Which letters and numbers look the same in a mirror as they do when they are written?

ꟼOTƧ

ƎƆИA⅃UᗺMA

How can you see yourself in the window at night?

During the day, people passing outside your window can look in and see you through the glass. This is because most of the light that hits you, bounces off you and goes out of the window into their eyes. But some of the light that hits you is reflected back into the room by the window.

During the day, you cannot see this reflected light because it is swamped by the large amounts of light coming from outside. At night, though, there is not any light coming from outside. So you can see the light reflected from the window. The glass acts like a mirror, allowing you to see a reflection of yourself.

The darker parts of the glass in this café window act like a mirror.

How does a pencil make a mark on paper?

Have you ever wondered how the writing stays on a piece of paper when you write with a pencil? Inside a pencil, there is a thin stick of a black substance, called graphite. We also call it pencil 'lead', although it has nothing to do with the metal called lead.

Graphite is made up of layers of tiny particles. As you write, you drag the pencil across the paper. A force called friction pulls the layers of graphite off the pencil and on to the paper. So the writing you see is actually a thin layer of graphite.

Friction is a force which makes two surfaces grip each other as they rub together. The rougher the surface, the more friction there is. If you try writing

Coloured pencils are made from graphite and clay. 'Lead' pencils also have clay in them.

on a very shiny surface, you will find that it does not work as well because there is less friction.

 Did you know?

Graphite is a form of **carbon**. Diamond is also a form of carbon. Graphite is quite soft but diamond is the hardest natural substance known.

Diamond can only be cut with diamond.

 Did you know?

Some 'lead' pencils are softer and darker than others. This is because they contain more graphite than the harder pencils, which have more clay. Letters and numbers on the side of a pencil show how soft and dark it is. H means that the pencil is hard and pale; B is soft and dark; HB is hard but dark.

 Did you know?

If you rub your hands together, the friction between them makes them feel warmer.

How does a magnet pick up pins?

If you spill some pins or needles on the floor, the best thing to use to pick them up is a magnet. The magnet pulls the pins towards it and makes them easier to collect.

A magnet produces an invisible force called a magnetic force. This attracts certain things towards it. It attracts iron or steel objects, such as pins, but not objects made of most other metals, paper, plastic, or rubber. The magnetic force works in an area around the magnet. This area is called the magnetic field. It is strongest at the far ends, or the north and south poles of the magnet. More pins will stick to the poles than to the rest of the magnet. There is a magnet in your fridge door which helps it to stick shut.

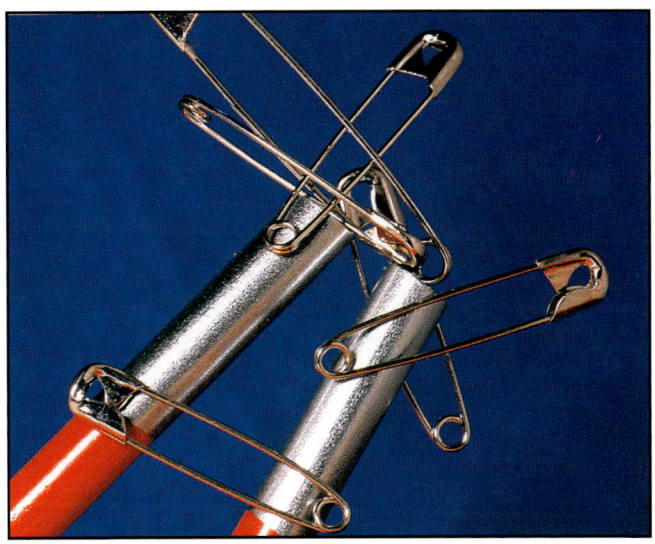
Safety pins clinging to a magnet.

 Did you know?

The Earth itself is a giant magnet. Its magnetic field reaches about 80,000 kilometres out into Space.

 See for yourself

Magnets have been used in compasses for thousands of years, because a magnet will always point to the north if it can swing freely. You can make a simple compass with a needle and some thread. Stroke the needle with a magnet 20 times, always stroking in the same direction. This will make the needle magnetic as well. Tie the thread around the middle of the needle and let it hang so that it is well balanced. The needle will swing and point to the north.

You can make a simple compass with a needle, some thread and a magnet.

How do kitchen scales work?

We use lots of different measuring instruments in the kitchen, including jugs, spoons and scales. When we weigh something on scales, we are actually measuring the effect that the force of gravity has on the mass of an object. The mass of an object is how much material the object contains.

Gravity is a force which pulls everything down towards the centre of the Earth. When it pulls down on an object's mass, it gives the object weight. We use scales to measure the weight of something.

There are different types of scales. Some use heavy weights, some use spring balances and others are electronic. In spring-balance scales, the weight of an object stretches the spring inside. This turns a wheel inside, making the outside pointer point to the correct weight.

 Did you know?

The mass of an object never changes, but its weight can. On the Moon, gravity is only a sixth as strong as on the Earth. So things have the same mass, but weigh only a sixth as much.

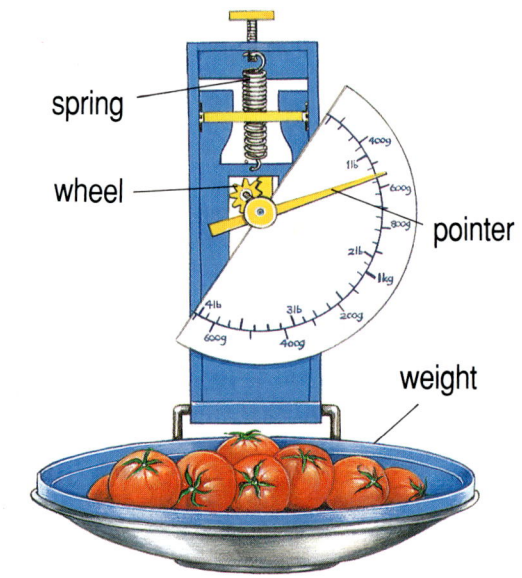

A pair of spring-balance scales.

Spring-balance scales being used in a vegetable market. This is one type of scale. When you go shopping see how many different kinds you can spot.

Try making your own set of scales. Stick a sheet of paper on the door, just under the door knob. Then hang a thin elastic band over the door knob. Tie a small carrier bag to the elastic band with some string. To work out a measuring scale, put marbles into the bag, five at a time. So the first time you will put five in the bag. The next you will put five more in to make ten, and so on. Mark on the paper where the bottom of the bag comes to each time. Then write the number of marbles next to each mark. When you have done this you can weigh other things, using marble measurements on a scale of 0, 5, 10, 15, 20 and so on.

Below right: Scales do not always use a pointer. Here, the weight is read on a screen.

Setting up your marble scales.

Above: These scales do not use a spring balance. Weights are used to balance the weight of the object that is put in the metal bowl.

What other ways can we weigh and measure things?

We weigh things in units called kilograms and grams. These belong to the metric system of measurement. In this system, kilometres, centimetres and millimetres are used to measure length, and litres and millilitres are used to measure **volume**.

When people first used units of measurement, they based them on different parts of the body. The Ancient Egyptians measured length in units called digits, palms and cubits. A digit equalled the length of a thumb. A palm equalled four digits. A cubit was the length from the elbow to the tip of the middle finger. It was equal to seven palms. Try measuring your bedroom in digits, palms and cubits.

What is the best way of cracking a nut?

We use lots of different machines and tools around our homes. Many of them make life easier for us. Some, such as washing machines and television sets, are very complicated. They use electricity to make them work. But other machines, such as nutcrackers, are much simpler. They use a person's own muscle power to make them work. But it is their design which makes cracking nuts easy.

Nutcrackers are examples of levers, which are some of the simplest types of machine. Some levers are used to move things. The simplest type is a long rod, which is propped up on a set point, called a fulcrum. The lever is used to move a heavy object, called a load. In order to do this, you have to push or pull the lever. This is called the effort. In a lever, the load is closer to the fulcrum than the effort is. You have to move the effort a long way to move the load a short way.

Hard nut shells can be cracked with little effort when nutcrackers are used.

Nutcrackers do not move loads, but they do make it much easier for you to break open nuts with hard shells. The nutcrackers are hinged at one end. This is the fulcrum. The nut is the load and the force you apply on the handles is the effort.

A simple lever

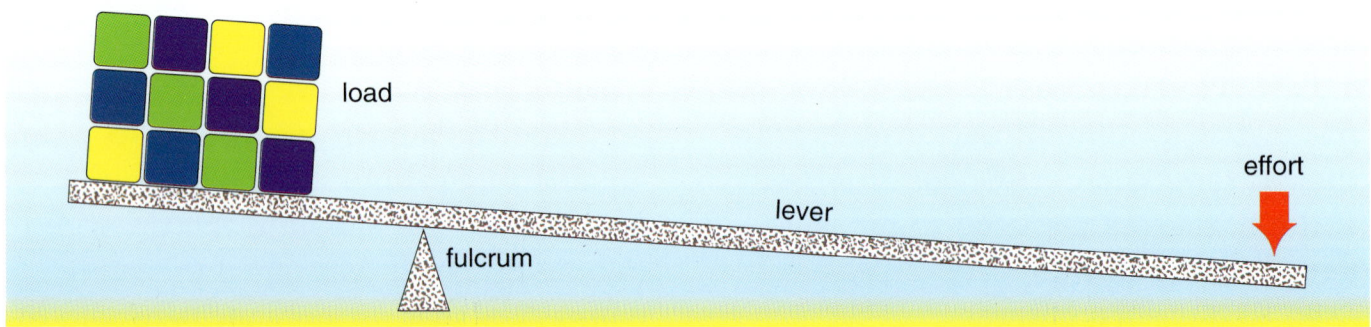

A small amount of effort can move a heavy load.

See for yourself

It is easier to move things with a longer lever. Try to **prise** the lid off a tin with a coin. Then try with the handle of a spoon. Which lever works best?

Which of these three levers will help best to open the tin?

Did you know?

There are lots of levers both indoors and outdoors. Many garden tools such as shears, wheelbarrows, forks and spades are levers.

A gardener using a fork as a lever to lift soil.

How do scissors cut paper?

Scissors are a type of lever. If you use the scissors to cut through paper, then the paper is the load. The fulcrum is where the two blades of the scissors are joined. You apply the effort at the handles. When you squeeze both of the handles towards each other, this pushes the blades together and they cut the paper. The closer to the fulcrum you put the paper, the easier it is to cut.

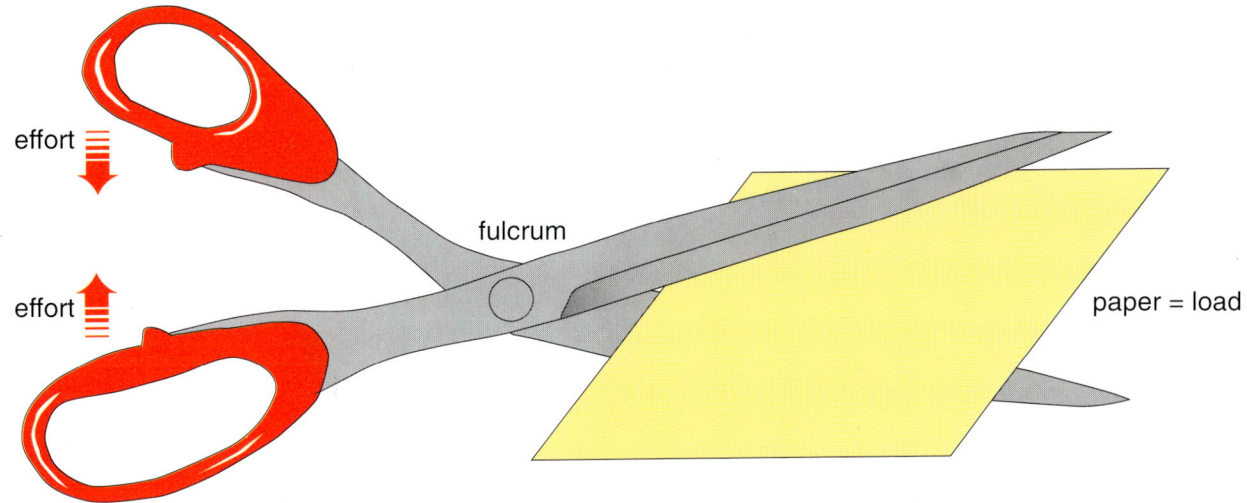

effort

fulcrum

effort

paper = load

To cut the paper, effort is applied to both handles.

How do clothes get dry in a spin dryer?

Things only move because there is a force pushing or pulling them along. They cannot move by themselves. You have already seen how some forces work, such as friction (see page 26), magnetism (see page 27) and gravity (see page 28). Forces can also change the speed at which something is moving. When things speed up, they are said to accelerate. When they slow down, they are said to decelerate.

If an object is pushed or pulled by a force, it starts moving in a straight line. But it can only change direction or go faster or slower if a different force acts on it. Things that move in a circle, such as wheels or spinning tops, are constantly changing direction in order to spin. They are also pulled by another force, called the centripetal force. This pulls the object towards the centre of the circle so that it keeps going round and round.

If you swing a bucketful of water round fast enough, the water will stay in the bucket. This is because of centripetal force. It keeps the water going round in a circle. If you do not swing the bucket fast enough, the water will spill out.

Centripetal force is used in spin dryers to force water out of wet clothes. The dryer spins wet clothes round very fast in a drum to get them dry. As the drum keeps spinning, the clothes inside it keep spinning too. The water is forced from them as they get flattened against the drum. It then flows out through hundreds of small holes in the drum's walls, and flows outside through a drainage pipe.

Dry clothes have stuck to the sides of the drum with the force of the spin.

Did you know?

If you swing something round in a circle, then let go, the object will always fly off in a straight line. Discus throwers and hammer throwers turn round to gather speed, but when they let go, the discus or hammer move in a straight line.

A hammer thrower spins round several times, getting faster and faster, before letting go of the hammer.

Did you know?

A roller coaster ride at a fair works by centripetal force. As the cars go round very fast in circles, centripetal force acts on them and presses the passengers back into their seats, so they never fall out.

The passengers are forced right back into their seats as they whirl round on the roller coaster.

See for yourself

There are several ways of seeing how centripetal force works. You could try spinning a bucketful of water round and round – but do this outside in the summer, and be prepared to get wet! Another experiment is to tie a cork to a piece of string and whirl it round you. Can you feel the force keeping the cork going round in a circle? Now let go. The cork will fly off in a straight line. Be careful when you do this – make sure you have plenty of room and that no one is close enough to get hit when the cork flies off.

What is fire?

When you see a candle flame or the flame on a gas cooker, you are watching a **chemical reaction**. Fire is very important in our lives. People cook with it, keep warm by it and use it to produce energy and power. But what is fire and why do things burn?

Fire is the light and heat which are given off when something burns. Things burst into flames when they reach a high enough temperature, called their ignition temperature. They burn because they **react** with oxygen in the air. Once something is alight, it

A burning gas flame.

makes so much heat of its own that it continues to burn.

A fire needs three things to keep it burning – fuel, heat and oxygen. If one

The flames of this house fire will be put out with jets of water. This takes the heat away.

of these things is taken away, the fire will go out. So, spraying fires with water takes the heat away and puts the fire out. Some fire extinguishers use foam to put fires out. The foam is sprayed on to the fire, smothering it and cutting off its oxygen supply. Foam is always used to smother and put out fires involving oil or petrol. Small foam extinguishers can be kept in the kitchen in case of fire.

All chemical reactions produce new materials. Burning produces ash and soot. It can also produce dangerous fumes. The scientific name for burning is combustion.

Why is a flame hot?

When a candle burns, it produces heat energy which makes it feel hot. It also produces light energy, which is why we can see the flame and why a candle lights up a room.

When the wick of a candle is lit, the heat melts the wax around it.

 Did you know?

Matches are often used for lighting fires. They work by friction (see page 26). When you strike a match on the side of a matchbox, the friction between the match and the box produces heat. This heat makes special chemicals in the matchhead burst into flames. The chemicals react with oxygen in the air and keep burning until you blow out the fire. Never play around with matches – they can be very dangerous.

 Did you know?

Rust is a chemical reaction as well. Things made of iron go rusty if they get wet or are left outside for a long time. The iron reacts with oxygen in the air, making a new brown material called rust. Many knives and forks are made of steel, which contains iron. But they do not go rusty because they also contain another metal called chromium, which protects them. This type of steel is called stainless steel.

These knives, forks and spoons will not rust because they are made of stainless steel.

Why does baking powder make cakes rise?

When you bake a cake, you often add some baking powder to make the cake rise. Baking powder is made of a chemical called sodium hydrogencarbonate. It is also known as sodium bicarbonate or bicarbonate of soda. When it is heated it gives off carbon dioxide gas. When you mix the ingredients of a cake and put them in the oven, you are in fact bringing about a chemical reaction. The heat releases bubbles of carbon dioxide from the baking powder, making your cake light and fluffy.

How does yeast make bread rise?

You can easily buy packets of dried yeast from a shop. But did you know that yeast is actually a type of fungus, belonging to the same group as mushrooms, toadstools and moulds? It is used in bread-making because, like baking powder, it gives off carbon dioxide. This makes the bread rise. Yeast contains certain chemicals, called enzymes. When bread is made, these enzymes react with sugar to break it down into carbon dioxide and other products.

Right: Cakes rise well when baking powder is used.

Below: These loaves have risen and are ready to be baked.

See for yourself

The best way of seeing how yeast works is to bake your own loaf of bread. You will need to ask an adult to help you.

1 Mix 2 teaspoonfuls of dried yeast with 1 teaspoonful of sugar in a mugful of warm water. Leave the mixture to stand for a few minutes until it becomes frothy. The froth is made up of bubbles of carbon dioxide.

2 Now mix 250 grams of strong bread flour with 2 teaspoonfuls of salt and a teaspoonful of butter.

3 Add the yeast mixture and mix the whole thing together with your hands

Kneading soft bread dough.

to form a dough. Knead it thoroughly, constantly pulling the dough apart with the palms of your hands and then folding it back again into a lump. This spreads the yeast evenly through the mixture.

4 Then cover the dough with a teacloth and leave it in a warm place for an hour. As the yeast continues to react, it will make the dough rise.

5 Knead the dough again, then place it in a greased loaf tin and let it rise once more.

6 Bake the dough in a hot oven (220 °C) for about 20 minutes or until the loaf sounds hollow when you tap it. Leave it to cool, then eat it!

The frothy yeast will be poured into the flour.

Why does food go mouldy?

Another type of fungus, called a mould, makes food go bad. It sometimes grows on old, stale bread or overripe fruit. Mould is made of tiny threads called hyphae. These spread all over the food, sucking the goodness out of it. They appear as a fluffy green or white covering. Some types of mould are used to treat many illnesses. Moulds are also put into some cheeses, such as blue cheeses, to make them tastier.

How does water pour from a tap?

When you turn on the kitchen tap, water comes pouring out because there is pressure pushing it. Pressure is another type of force (see pages 26-28). This force pushes, or presses on something, and works best when it is applied downwards. This is because the force is being helped by the Earth's gravity, which pulls everything down towards it, even you.

With liquids, such as water, pressure increases as the depth of the water increases. If you have a deep tank of water, the water will flow out of the bottom much faster than out of the top. This is because all the water above it pushes it out.

The higher the tank is, the greater the pressure and the faster the water will come out of the tap. Most houses have their water tanks in the roof – the highest place in the house. When you turn on the tap, water flows quickly downwards from the tank in the roof to the tap. It is pushed out through the tap by the weight of water above it.

Water flowing from a tap.

⚠ See for yourself

To see water pressure in action, you will need an empty washing-up liquid bottle and some sticky tape. Punch a line of small holes down one side of the bottle. Cover them with tape. Now fill the bottle with water. Peel the tape off. From which hole is the most water pouring out?

The holes must be covered with the sticky tape before water is poured into the bottle.

How does a siphon work?

You can move water from a high place to a low place without having to pour it. Instead, you can use a tube-like device called a siphon. First the water is sucked along the tube out of the higher container. Then it runs down into the lower container. It works because the water is pushed along the tube by the pressure of the water in the higher container above it. The end of the tube where the water pours out, is lower than the end that is stuck in the higher container.

Why do houses get draughty?

Hold a feather or a tissue by the side of a window or at the bottom of a door. Is there a draught blowing through? Draughts are caused by differences in air pressure inside the house. Like water, air has pressure as well. It presses down on everything, including you. But you do not normally feel it because your body is designed to balance it out. When air presses hard, there is high pressure. When it presses down more softly, there is low pressure.

Air blows through a crack from high air pressure outside, to low air pressure inside.

Why do doors slam shut on their own?

If you leave a door or a window open in your house, another door may suddenly slam shut. It seems to shut by itself. In fact, it shuts because of differences in air pressure. Winds and draughts are moving air. If there is a window or door open, the air flows around the house. When it blows into a room, the air pressure in the room is higher than it is outside. If the door of the room is open, some of the air then tries to flow outside again to even up the pressure. As it does so, it pushes against the door and makes it shut.

When this door is shut properly, it fits close to the door frame to stop draughts.

How does a vacuum cleaner suck up dirt?

Vacuum cleaners also work because of differences in air pressure. An electric motor turns a fan inside the cleaner. It blows air out of the cleaner, lowering the pressure inside it. Air is then sucked in through the front of the vacuum cleaner to balance out the pressure. Inside it flows through a bag, which is full of tiny holes, like a filter. They allow air to flow out again, but trap any dust and dirt that has got sucked in with the air.

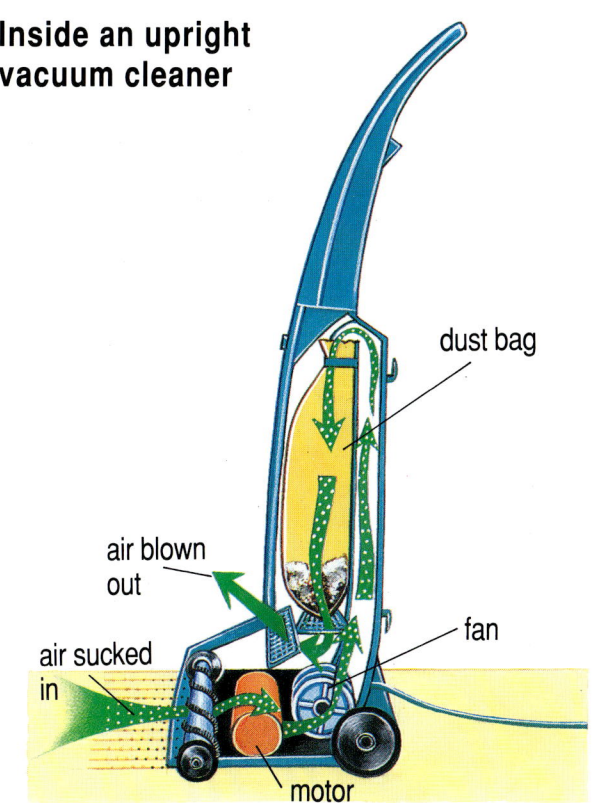

Inside an upright vacuum cleaner

dust bag

air blown out

air sucked in

fan

motor

This is a cylinder vacuum cleaner. Air and dirt are sucked up through a hose.

Why does wind howl down the chimney?

When the wind blows across the top of an open chimney top, it makes the air inside the chimney stack vibrate. Sound is made when air vibrates (see page 22). These vibrations cause the howling sound that you hear. If you blow gently across the top of a glass bottle, it will make a whistling sound in the same way as a chimney does.

 ## See for yourself

To see the effects of air pressure, you will need a large plastic drinks' bottle. The pressure of the air inside the bottle gives the bottle its shape. Try sucking some of the air out of the bottle. The bottle will start to collapse as the air pressure inside it is reduced.

Open chimney tops make the wind whistle inside.

How does heat travel around your house?

Heat always moves from hotter to colder things, but it travels around your house in three different ways. These are called convection, conduction and radiation. Heat moves through solid objects by conduction. So, if you leave a metal spoon in a bowl of hot soup, the spoon will get hot as heat travels through it by conduction. It travels more easily through some materials than through others. Heat travels easily through metals, so these are good conductors. Materials such as wood, cork or plastic are poor conductors. Saucepans often have wood or plastic handles so that you do not burn yourself when you pick them up. Table mats can be made of cork to stop hot plates and pots from burning the table. Now look carefully at the picture below. Why do all these implements need to be made partly from materials which are bad conductors?

How do radiators warm the room?

Radiators are full of water, which heats up when you turn the central heating system on. The hot water heats up the metal of the radiator, making the air around it hotter. Heat travels from a radiator by convection. This is how heat travels through gases, such as air, or liquids. The hot air around the radiator rises, because the air molecules spread out as they are heated, making the air lighter. The warmth is carried around the room as the air spreads. Cold air is heavier than hot air. It sinks to replace the hot air. The radiator then heats this cold air, which in turn rises, and so the **cycle** carries on.

This is how the radiator's heat is spread around the room. The moving

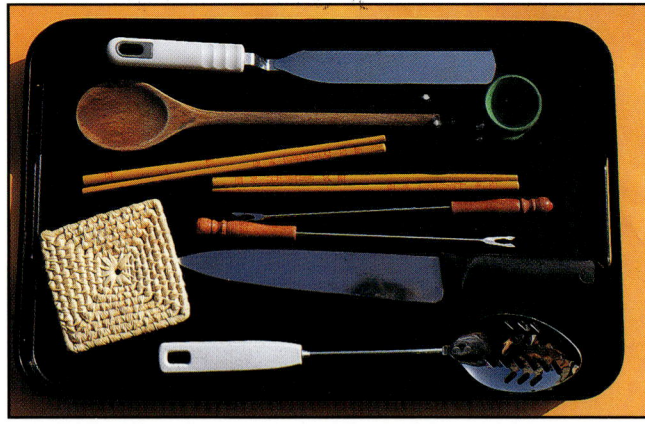

Can you name the good and bad conductors in this picture?

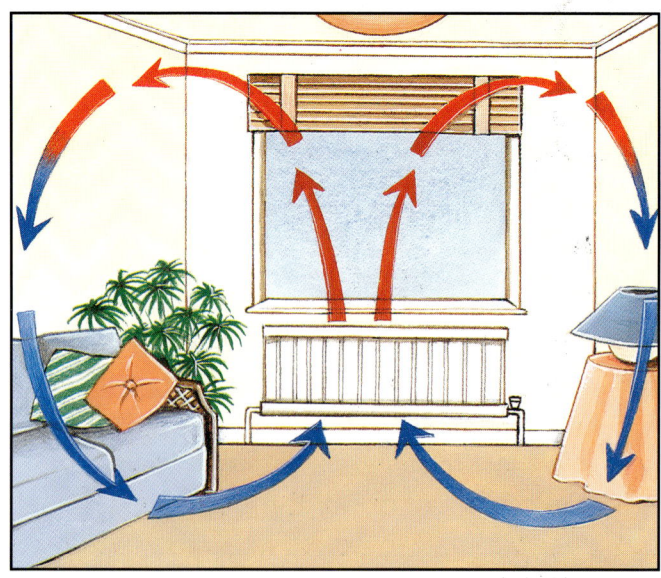

Warm air rises from the radiator and is replaced by cold air.

air is called a convection current. Heat can also spread by radiation. This is when it travels in invisible straight lines called rays. The heat from an open wood or coal fire spreads out in this way.

Did you know?

Space is completely empty, so heat cannot travel through it by conduction or convection. The Sun's heat and light reach us by radiation.

Why do radiators gurgle?

In a central heating system, a boiler heats up the water, which is piped round the house to the radiators. The radiators or pipes sometimes make a gurgling sound. This is because bubbles of air get trapped in the water inside them. As the bubbles move, they make a gurgling noise. To stop the noise, you have to use a special key to let the air out of the radiators.

See for yourself

To see how hot air rises, hold a piece of tissue paper above a radiator. The tissue will flutter in the convection current. Now cut out a spiral of paper and thread a piece of cotton through it. You will see the spiral twirl round as you hold it over the radiator.

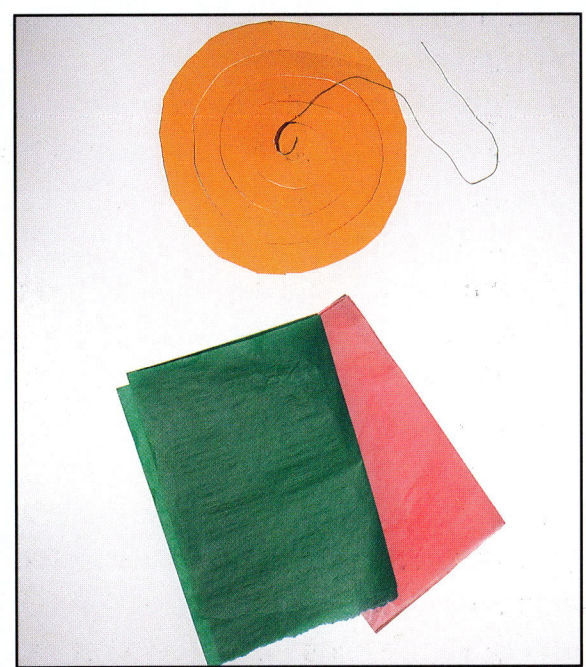

Soft tissue paper and a spiral which will unravel when it is lifted up by the cotton.

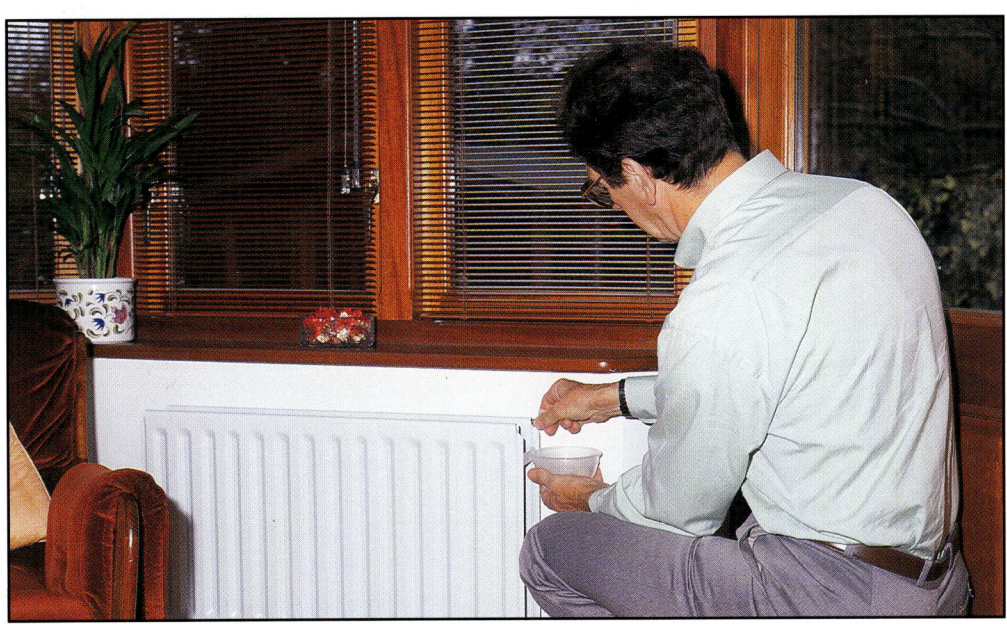

This man is letting trapped air out of a radiator. He is holding a cup underneath to catch water, which will come out with the air.

How does a duvet keep you warm?

Materials that stop heat escaping are called insulators. Heat cannot travel through them. Air is a good insulator. This means that materials which trap air, such as woollen clothes, are also good insulators.

At night, your body gives out heat which warms the air around you. This warm air drifts upwards and is replaced by cool air, which your body then heats up. This heat is travelling by convection (see page 42). But not all the warmth escapes. If it did, you would get very cold. The fluffy fibres in the duvet have pockets of air between them. Your body heats this air, and the fibres trap it so it cannot escape. The duvet also blocks the cool air coming towards you. Now you can see why layers of thin blankets will keep you warmer than one thick blanket. They trap a lot of warm air between the layers.

Why does double glazing keep in the warmth?

A lot of heat is lost from houses through the windows, walls and roof. People put double glazing on their windows to stop too much heat escaping. A layer of air is trapped between the two sheets of glass. The heat would need to pass through the inner pane of glass, the layer of air, and then the outer pane of glass.

Another way of insulating a house is to fill any **cavity walls** with foam. This traps bubbles of air between the two layers of brick and stops the heat escaping.

Fast asleep under a warm duvet.

The gap between the walls will be filled with foam.

How does a vacuum flask keep things hot or cold?

A vacuum flask keeps hot drinks hot and cold drinks cold. It does this by stopping heat travelling in and out through the flask walls. Inside a flask, there is a special container made of two thin layers of silver-coated glass. The area between the two layers is a vacuum. This means that there is nothing in it, not even air. Heat cannot travel through a vacuum, so it cannot enter or escape by convection or conduction (see page 42). But it could enter or escape by radiation (see pages 42 and 43). This is why the container

is coated in silver. Any heat that is radiated through is reflected back again by the silver coating. The silver coating acts a bit like a mirror (see pages 24-25).

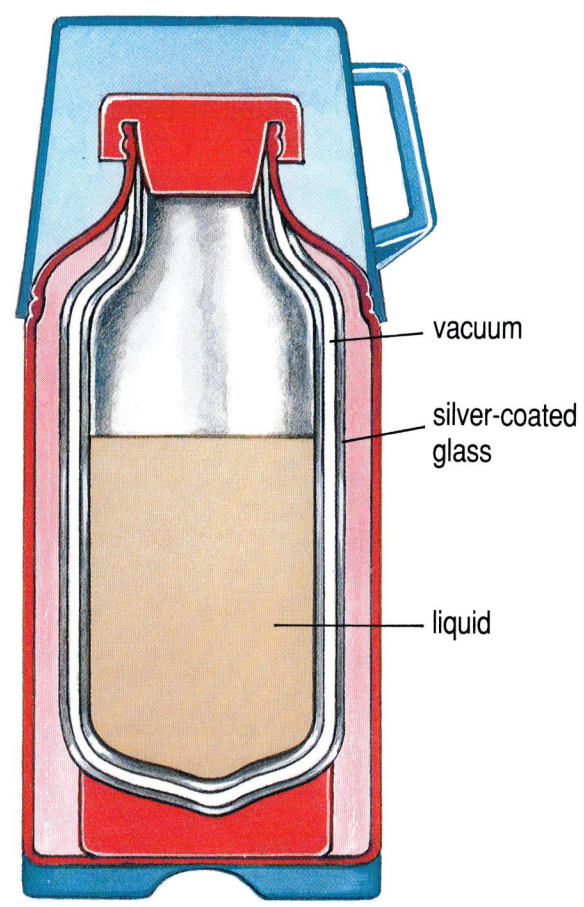

vacuum

silver-coated glass

liquid

Neither heat nor cold are able to pass through the vacuum.

These colourful flasks keep drinks either hot or cold.

Glossary

appliance a useful piece of equipment

bonds connections; links

carbon a natural substance that is made from plant matter and is found in rock; there are many forms of carbon, from coal to diamonds

cavity walls double walls with an empty space, or cavity, between them

chemical reaction any change within a substance which alters its chemicals; or a change that makes it into a different substance

cycle a series of changes that keeps repeating itself

decreases gets less

fibres fine threads

image a picture or likeness of something

prise to force open with a lever

react to respond or change as a result of coming into contact with something different

taut tight and straight

vapour the gas form of a liquid

vibrates moves backwards and forwards very quickly

volume the amount of space that something takes up

Books to read

Electricity and Magnetism Kay Davies and Wendy Oldfield (Wayland)
How Science Works Judith Hann (Dorling Kindersley)
Finding Out About Things at Home E Humberstone (Usborne)
Science Encyclopedia (Kingfisher)
How Things Work Brian Knapp (Atlantic Europe)
Dictionary of Science Stockley, Oxlade, Wertheim (Usborne)